Introduction

Presenting Poetry provides the basis of a number of poetry sessions for primary classes (approximately 8- to 12-year-olds). The units contain:

1. a group of poems linked by a common theme, structure or feature;
2. some questions about the poems, designed to help pupils get the most out of their reading;
3. one or more follow-up activities, for example art or craft work, drama, discussion, music, recitation, choral presentation or poetry writing. These activities are often non-written and intended to show poetry as linked to the aesthetic and expressive arts.

A typical poetry session might take the following shape:

1. re-reading together of a poem or poems enjoyed in a previous session;
2. time for pupils to choose and read for pleasure, with the group, some of their favourite poems;
3. a detailed look at one unit, and follow-up work related to it. The book can, of course, also be used more informally in odd moments as a poetry anthology.

Reading the poems

When pupils meet each poem for the first time, it should be through the teacher's reading, because a well-read rendering maximises the listener's pleasure. It is strongly recommended, therefore, that teachers *practise* each poem before reading it aloud for the first time to the class. Later on, the pupils should have an opportunity to read aloud themselves. If the teacher has provided a good example of how to handle rhythm, rhyme, dramatic effects, etc., the pupil's task will be easier and more pleasurable. The pupil will also have been introduced to new or difficult words or ideas.

After this first teacher-reading of the poem, the pupil's understanding should be ensured through discussion based on the comprehension questions in the text. A second teacher-reading of the poem is often a good idea, before handing over to pupil-readers.

Although comprehension questions are included, full comprehension by all pupils of all poems is not always possible – nor is it essential. Children are well used to coping with half-grasped ideas, and may enjoy the sounds and images of the more difficult poems for their own sake.

It is recommended that all pupil-readers be volunteers and that no pupil be forced to read. It is best to choose competent volunteers first and less competent ones later on when they have had a chance to become more familiar with words and rhythms from several hearings. It is worth trying a wide range of reading methods: single voice reading, paired reading, group reading, choral reading, and combinations of these. Happy chanting (where appropriate) is not to be despised: it gives pleasure and helps commit poems to memory. When possible and practical, children may be encouraged to use sound effects, music, etc., to accompany their readings.

Follow-up

Any follow-up work should be varied and pleasurable. Some poetry writing is included as part of a balanced follow-up programme. Unit poems are often used as a model for the pupil's work, since this is an effective way of starting children off on their own poetry writing. Learning poetry by heart is a useful memory-training exercise and can provide great pleasure. Children should be encouraged to learn their favourite poems by heart every now and then. Often poems are picked up effortlessly if they are read aloud frequently. The prospect of an audience motivates children's performance enormously. Try to provide an audience – another class, the school – for their presentations.

Contents

PRESENTING
POETRY 4

PATRICIA McCALL, SUE PALMER
AND GORDON JARVIE

Hodder & Stoughton
A MEMBER OF THE HODDER HEADLINE GROUP

Illustrations by Ian Andrew, Shirley Bellwood, Linda Birch, Francis
Blake, Margaret Chamberlain, Rowan Clifford, John Fardell, Sheila
Galbraith, John Harrold, Thelma Lambert, John Marshall, Steve
Smallman and Guy Smith

First edition published 1986 by Oliver & Boyd

British Library Cataloguing in Publication Data
A catalogue record for this title is available from The British Library

ISBN 0 340 67008 8

First published 1986 by Oliver & Boyd
Revised edition 1996 Hodder & Stoughton
Impression number   10 9 8 7 6 5 4 3 2 1
Year   1999 1988 1997 1996

Copyright © 1996 Hodder & Stoughton

Typeset by Hewer Text Composition Services, Edinburgh.
Printed in Hong Kong for Hodder & Stoughton Educational,
a division of Hodder Headline Plc, 338 Euston Road, London
NW1 3BH by Colorcraft Ltd, Hong Kong.

There was a young bard of Japan

There was a young lady of Riga
Who went for a ride on a tiger;
They finished the ride
With the lady inside,
And a smile on the face of the tiger.

No one knows who invented the limerick. This form of writing goes back many centuries; even Shakespeare wrote verses that sound like limericks.
The verse-form gets its name from the town of Limerick in Ireland, where limericks used to be sung by the soldiers of the Irish Brigade. It was first made popular by the Victorian poet, Edward Lear. Here is one of Lear's most famous limericks:

There was a young lady whose chin
Resembled the point of a pin;
So she had it made sharp
And purchased a harp,
And played several tunes with her chin.

Try tapping out the rhythm of this limerick while someone reads it aloud.
Since Edward Lear first made limericks popular, many have been written, always with five lines, always funny and usually starting with the words,
"There was a young/old ____ of ____".

Try tapping out the rhythm of the next one:

There was an old lady of Ryde
Who ate some green apples and died.
The apples fermented
Inside the lamented—
Made cider inside 'er inside.

Compare the rhythms of Lear's limerick and the last one. Can you hear that they are the same?
This rhythm is one of the special features of the limerick. Listen to the rhythm in the next two.

There was an old man of Darjeeling
Who travelled from London to Ealing.
It said on the door
"Please don't spit on the floor."
So he carefully spat on the ceiling.

There was a young lady of Twickenham
Whose shoes were too tight to walk quick in 'em;
She came back from a walk
Looking whiter than chalk,
And took 'em both off and was sick in 'em.

Limericks also have a special rhyme-scheme:

There was an old fellow of Tring	**A**
Who, when someone asked him to sing,	**A**
Replied, "Ain't it odd?	**B**
I can never tell God	**B**
Save the Weasel from Pop goes the King."	**A**

The rhyme pattern of this limerick has been marked, using letters.
Tring gets an A because it is the first rhyming word. *Sing* gets an A also, because it rhymes with *Tring*.
Odd gets a B because it comes next but does not rhyme with *Tring* or *sing*. *God* gets a B also because it rhymes with *odd*.
Last of all, *King* gets an A because it rhymes with *Tring* and *sing*.
So the rhyme pattern, or rhyme scheme, is:

A
A
B
B
A

Look at the next two limericks and check to see if they follow this rhyme scheme.

> There was a young girl of Asturias
> Whose temper was frantic and furious.
> She used to throw eggs
> At her grandmother's legs—
> A habit unpleasant, but curious.

> There was a young lady of Spain
> Who was dreadfully sick on a train,
> Not once, but again
> And again and again
> And again and again and again.

Can you work this one out?

> She frowned and called him Mr.
> Because in sport he kr.
> And so, in spite,
> That very night,
> This Mr. kr. sr.

ACTIVITY: Limerick Writing

Try writing a limerick for yourself.
Remember:
1) Five lines
2) Special rhythm
3) A A B B A rhyme scheme.
4) The first line usually begins, "There was a young/old ____ of ____."
5) It should be funny.

Special hints:
1) Work out your rhyming words first.
2) Test your limerick and its rhythm by reading it aloud.
3) If the rhythm doesn't fit (or 'scan') change some words about until it does.

UNIT TWO

War

During the Crimean War in the 1850's, a brigade of British cavalry (The Light Brigade) were given wrong directions in a battle. They found themselves charging into a valley, directly at the enemy guns. Obedient to orders, however, they did not retreat. They galloped right up to the guns, and charged at them with sabres. Of six hundred men who took part in this charge, fewer than two hundred survived. A poem was written by Alfred, Lord Tennyson, the Poet Laureate at the time, honouring their bravery.

Balaclava: The Charge of the Light Brigade

The Charge of the Light Brigade

Half a league, half a league,
  Half a league onward,
All in the valley of Death,
  Rode the six hundred.
'Forward the Light Brigade!
Charge for the guns!' he said:
Into the valley of Death
  Rode the six hundred.

'Forward the Light Brigade!'
Was there a man dismay'd?
Not though the soldier knew
  Someone had blunder'd:
Theirs not to make reply,
Theirs not to reason why,
Theirs but to do and die:
Into the valley of Death
  Rode the six hundred.

Cannon to right of them,
Cannon to left of them,
Cannon in front of them
  Volley'd and thunder'd;
Stormed at with shot and shell,
Boldly they rode and well,
Into the jaws of Death,
Into the mouth of Hell
  Rode the six hundred.

Flash'd all their sabres bare,
Flash'd as they turn'd in air
Sabring the gunners there,
Charging an army, while

All the world wonder'd:
Plunged in the battery-smoke
Right through the line they broke;
Cossack and Russian
Reel'd from the sabre-stroke
   Shatter'd and sunder'd.
Then they rode back, but not
   Not the six hundred.

Cannon to right of them,
Cannon to left of them,
Cannon behind them
   Volley'd and thunder'd
Storm'd at with shot and shell,
While horse and hero fell,
They that had fought so well
Came thro' the jaws of Death,
Back from the mouth of Hell,
All that was left of them,
   Left of six hundred.

When can their glory fade?
O the wild charge they made!
   All the world wonder'd.
Honour the charge they made!
Honour the Light Brigade,
   Noble six hundred!

Alfred, Lord Tennyson

This poem is a good one for reading in unison because the rhythm is so strong. Try reading it in groups, one group per stanza.
Did the soldiers know that the charge was a mistake? (Look at the second stanza.)

Officers of the 42nd Highlanders, Black Watch in the Crimea

Do you think what they did was glorious? Why or why not?
What is a Poet Laureate?
The next two poems were written about sixty years later, during World War I (1914–1918), by soldiers serving on the British side.
The first ends with a Latin quotation, *Dulce et decorum est pro patria mori*. This was sometimes written on soldiers' graves and means, "It is sweet and fitting to die for your country". (You pronounce it "dul-kay et deck-orum est pro patria mor-ee.")

Dulce Et Decorum Est

Bent double, like old beggars under sacks,
Knock-kneed, coughing like hags, we cursed through sludge,
Till on the haunting flares we turned our backs,
And towards our distant rest began to trudge.
Men marched asleep. Many had lost their boots,
But limped on, blood-shod. All went lame, all blind;
Drunk with fatigue; deaf even to the hoots
Of gas-shells dropping softly behind.

Gas! GAS! Quick, boys!—An ecstasy of fumbling,
Fitting the clumsy helmets just in time,
But someone still was yelling out and stumbling
And floundering like a man in fire or lime—
Dim through the misty panes and thick green light,
As under a green sea, I saw him drowning.
In all my dreams before my helpless sight
He plunges at me, guttering, choking, drowning.

If in some smothering dreams, you too could pace
Behind the wagon that we flung him in,
And watch the white eyes writhing in his face,
His hanging face, like a devil's sick of sin;
If you could hear, at every jolt, the blood
Come gargling from the froth-corrupted lungs,
Bitter as the cud
Of vile, incurable sores on innocent tongues,—
My friend, you would not tell with such high zest
To children ardent for some desperate glory,
The old lie: Dulce et decorum est
Pro patria mori.

Wilfred Owen

What are the soldiers doing in the first stanza?
What sort of condition are they in?
What do they do when they hear the gas
shells? Why does the poet see the dying man
through misty panes and thick green light?
Read the poem again, and work out whom the
poet is addressing at the end.
Do you think Wilfred Owen believes that it is
sweet and fitting to die for your country? Give
reasons for your answer.

In the trenches, World War I

British soldiers firing into dugouts, World War I

The next poem was also written by a soldier, Siegfried Sassoon.

The General

"Good morning, good morning!" the General said
When we met him last week on our way to the line.
Now the soldiers he smiled at are most of 'em dead
And we're cursing his staff for incompetent swine.
"He's a cheery old card," grunted Harry to Jack
As they slogged up to Arras with rifle and pack.

But he did for them both with his plan of attack.

What does *incompetent* (line 4) mean?
What happened to Harry and Jack in the end?
Whose fault does the poet think it was?

Read all the poems aloud again.
Which do you like best? Why?

How does Lord Tennyson's attitude to war
differ from that of Owen and Sassoon?
Why do you think this is?
Which attitude do you agree with, and why?
Is it possible to like one of the poems without
agreeing with the poet's attitude?

UNIT THREE

Charles Causley

Charles Causley was born in 1917 in Launceston, Cornwall, where he still lives. He wasn't very interested in poetry at school – "It never occurred to me to write a poem at school unless I was asked to by a teacher." When he left school he worked for a builder and played the piano in a small dance band for some years. During the Second World War, he joined the Navy and it was while serving on the destroyer *Eclipse*, in Scapa Flow in Orkney, that he first began to write poetry. He wrote his first real poem in 1943 when he was 26. After the war, Charles Causley left the Navy and went home to Cornwall to become a teacher and a poet. He has since written many poems, all of them interesting and varied as you will see.

The first Charles Causley poem in this unit is a funny one – but one with a serious message.

I Saw a Jolly Hunter

I saw a jolly hunter
  With a jolly gun
Walking in the country
  In the jolly sun.

In the jolly meadow
  Sat a jolly hare.
Saw the jolly hunter.
  Took jolly care.

Hunter jolly eager—
  Sight of jolly prey.
Forgot gun pointing
  Wrong jolly way.

Jolly hunter jolly head
  Over heels gone.
Jolly old safety-catch
  Not jolly on.

Bang went the jolly gun.
  Hunter jolly dead.
Jolly hare got clean away.
  Jolly good, I said.

Charles Causley

With whom do you sympathise – the hunter or the hare? Why?
The next poem is rather weird and creepy.

Infant Song

Don't you love my baby, mam,
Lying in his little pram,

Polished all with water clean,
The finest baby ever seen?

Daughter, daughter, if I could
I'd love your baby as I should,

But why the suit of signal red,
The horns that grow out of his head,

Why does he burn with brimstone heat,
Have cloven hooves instead of feet,

Fishing hooks upon each hand,
The keenest tail that's in the land,

Pointed ears and teeth so stark
And eyes that flicker in the dark?

Don't you love my baby, mam?

Dearest, I do not think I can.
I do not, do not think I can.

                    Charles Causley

Could you have loved the baby?

My Neighbour Mr Normanton

My neighbour Mr. Normanton
Who lives at ninety-five
'S as typical an Englishman
As any one alive.

He wears pin-stripes and bowler-hat.
His accent is sublime.
He keeps a British bull-dog
And British Summer Time.

His shoes are always glassy black
(He never wears the brown);
His brolly's rolled slim as a stick
When he goes up to town,

He much prefers a game of darts
To mah-jong or to chess.
He fancies Chelsea for the Cup
And dotes on G. & S.

Roast beef and Yorkshire pudding are
What he most likes to eat.
His drinks are tea and British beer
And sometimes whisky (neat).

Out of a British briar-pipe
He puffs an Empire smoke
While gazing at his roses (red)
Beneath a British oak.

And in his British garden
Upon St. George's Day
He hoists a British Union Jack
And shouts, 'Hip, hip, hooray!'

But tell me, Mr. Normanton,
That evening after dark,
Who were those foreign gentlemen
You met in Churchill Park?

You spoke a funny language
I couldn't understand;
And wasn't that some microfilm
You'd hidden in your hand?

And then that note I saw you post
Inside a hollow tree!
When I jumped out you turned about
As quick as quick could be.

Why did you use a hearing-aid
While strolling in the park
And talking to that worried-looking
Admiralty clerk?

The day you took the cypher-book
From underneath a stone,
I'm certain, Mr. Normanton,
You thought you were alone.

Your powerful transmitter!
The stations that you call!
I love to watch you through the crack
That's in my bedroom wall.

Oh, thank you, Mr. Normanton,
For asking me to tea.
It's really all quite rivetting
To clever chaps like me.

What? Will I come and work for you?
Now please don't mention pay.

What super luck I left a note
To say I'd run away!

Is that a gun that's in your hand?
And look! A lethal pill!
And that's a real commando-knife?
I say, this is a thrill!

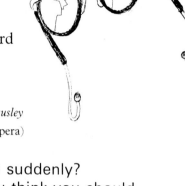

Of course I've never said a word
About the things you do.
Let's keep it all a secret
Between just me and . . .

Charles Causley

G & S – Gilbert and Sullivan (light opera)

Why does the poem end so suddenly?
In what sort of voice do you think you should
read this poem? Try to work out a voice which
really suits the character of the boy who is
talking. Now let someone read the poem again
using this voice. Be sure to break off in a really
dramatic way at the end.

The fourth poem is a rather strange, but very
beautiful one. It is meant to have been written
by the ghost of a young cowboy. Because it is
quite hard to understand, some explanatory
footnotes have been added to help you.
However, with poems like this it doesn't really
matter whether you understand every word or
not. You can enjoy the sounds and the pictures
which the poem conjures up anyway.

Cowboy Song

I come from Salem County
    Where the silver melons grow,
Where the wheat is sweet as an angel's feet
    And the zithering zephyrs blow. (1)
I walk the blue bone-orchard (2)
    In the apple-blossom snow,
When the teasy bees take their honeyed ease
    And the marmalade moon hangs low.

My Maw sleeps prone on the prairie
    In a boulder eiderdown, (3)
Where the pickled stars in their little jam-jars
    Hang in a hoop to town.
I haven't seen Paw since a Sunday
    In eighteen seventy-three
When he packed his snap in a bitty mess-trap (4)
    And said he'd be home by tea.

Fled is my fancy sister
    All weeping like a willow.
And dead is the brother I loved like no other
    Who once did share my pillow.
I fly the florid water
    Where run the seven geese round,
O the townsfolk talk to see me walk
    Six inches off the ground.

Across the map of midnight
    I trawl the turning sky,
In my green glass the salt fleets pass,
    The moon her fire-float by.

The girls go gay in the valley
    When the boys come down from the farm,
Don't run, my joy, from a poor cowboy,
    I won't do you no harm.

The bread of my twentieth birthday
    I buttered with the sun,
Though I sharpen my eyes with lovers' lies
    I'll never see twenty-one.
Light is my shirt with lilies,
    And lined with lead my hood,
On my face as I pass is a plate of brass, (5)
    And my suit is made of wood.

Charles Causley

(1) gentle winds
(2) grave-yard   (4) packed his lunch in a tin
(3) the boulder is her grave-stone   (5) he is in his coffin

ACTIVITY I: Painting

Choose one of the poems to paint. It is best to read them over again to yourself and choose the one which gives you the most vivid pictures in your mind.

ACTIVITY 2: Setting Words to Music

Choose one of the poems and try to set it to a tune you already know (e.g. *Cowboy Song* fits well to "Oh Susannah" and *My Neighbour Mr Normanton* fits to "Clementine").
You could even make up a tune yourself and accompany the poem on the chime bars or glockenspiel.

Ripping Yarns

Both the poems in this unit are what used to be called "rattling good stories". They both have strong rhyme and rhythm and canter along at a racy pace. Enjoy them!

The Green Eye of the Yellow God

There's a one-eyed yellow idol to the north of Khatmandu,
There's a little marble cross below the town;
There's a broken-hearted woman tends the grave of Mad Carew,
And the Yellow God forever gazes down.

He was known as "Mad Carew" by the subs at Khatmandu,
He was hotter than they felt inclined to tell;
But for all his foolish pranks, he was worshipped in the ranks,
And the Colonel's daughter smiled on him as well.

He had loved her all along, with the passion of the strong,
The fact that she loved him was plain to all.
She was nearly twenty-one and arrangements had begun
To celebrate her birthday with a ball.

He wrote to ask what present she would like from Mad Carew;
They met next day as he dismissed a squad;
And jestingly she told him then that nothing else would do
But the green eye of the little Yellow God.

On the night before the dance, Mad Carew seemed in a trance,
And they chaffed him as they puffed at their cigars;
But for once he failed to smile, and he sat alone awhile,
Then went out into the night beneath the stars.

He returned before the dawn, with his shirt and tunic torn,
And a gash across his temple dripping red;
He was patched up right away, and he slept through all the day,
And the Colonel's daughter watched beside his bed.

He woke at last and asked if they could send his tunic through;
She brought it, and he thanked her with a nod;
He bade her search the pocket saying, "That's from Mad Carew",
And she found the little green eye of the god.

She upbraided poor Carew in the way that women do,
Though both her eyes were strangely hot and wet;
But she wouldn't take the stone and Mad Carew was left alone
With the jewel that he'd chanced his life to get.

When the ball was at its height, on that still and tropic night,
She thought of him and hastened to his room;
As she crossed the barrack square she could hear the dreamy air
Of a waltz tune softly stealing thro' the gloom.

His door was open wide, with silver moonlight shining through;
The place was wet and slipp'ry where she trod;
An ugly knife lay buried in the heart of Mad Carew,
'Twas the "Vengeance of the Little Yellow God".

There's a one-eyed yellow idol to the north of Khatmandu,
There's a little marble cross below the town;
There's a broken-hearted woman tends the grave of Mad Carew,
And the Yellow God forever gazes down.

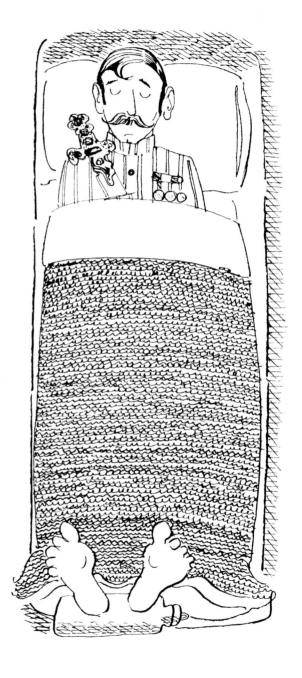

J. Milton Hayes

The Cremation of Sam McGee

There are strange things done in the midnight sun
  By the men who moil for gold;
The Arctic trails have their secret tales
  That would make your blood run cold;
The Northern Lights have seen queer sights,
  But the queerest they ever did see
Was that night on the marge of Lake Lebarge
  I cremated Sam McGee.

Now Sam McGee was from Tennessee, where the cotton blooms and blows.
Why he left his home in the South to roam 'round the Pole, God only knows.
He was always cold, but the land of gold seemed to hold him like a spell;
Though he'd often say in his homely way that "he'd sooner live in hell."

On a Christmas Day we were mushing our way over the Dawson trail.
Talk of your cold! through the parka's fold it stabbed like a driven nail.
If our eyes we'd close, then the lashes froze till sometimes we couldn't see;
It wasn't much fun, but the only one to whimper was Sam McGee.

And that very night, as we lay packed tight in our robes beneath the snow,
And the dogs were fed, and the stars o'erhead were dancing heel and toe,
He turned to me, and "Cap," says he, "I'll cash in this trip, I guess;
And if I do, I'm asking that you won't refuse my last request."

Well, he seemed so low that I couldn't say no; then he says with a sort of moan:
'It's the cursèd cold, and it's got right hold till I'm chilled clean through to the bone.
Yet 'tain't being dead—it's my awful dread of the icy grave that pains;
So I want you to swear that, foul or fair, you'll cremate my last remains."

A pal's last need is a thing to heed, so I swore I would not fail;
And we started on at the streak of dawn; but God! he looked ghastly pale.
He crouched on the sleigh, and he raved all day of his home in Tennessee;
And before nightfall a corpse was all that was left of Sam McGee.

There wasn't a breath in that land of death, and I hurried, horror-driven,
With a corpse half hid that I couldn't get rid, because of a promise given;
It was lashed to the sleigh, and it seemed to say: "You may tax your brawn and brains,
But you promised true, and it's up to you to cremate those last remains."

Now a promise made is a debt unpaid, and the trail has its own stern code.
In the days to come, though my lips were dumb, in my heart how I cursed that load.
In the long, long night, by the lone firelight, while the huskies, round in a ring,
Howled out their woes to the homeless snows—O God! how I loathed the thing.

And every day that quiet clay seemed to heavy and heavier grow;
And on I went, though the dogs were spent and the grub was getting low;
The trail was bad, and I felt half mad, but I swore I would not give in;
And I'd often sing to the hateful thing, and it hearkened with a grin.

Till I came to the marge of Lake Lebarge, and a derelict there lay;
It was jammed in the ice, but I saw in a trice it was called the "Alice May."
And I looked at it, and I thought a bit, and I looked at my frozen chum;
Then "Here," said I, with a sudden cry, "is my cre-ma-tor-eum."

Some planks I tore from the cabin floor, and I lit the boiler fire;
Some coal I found that was lying around, and I heaped the fuel higher;
The flames just soared, and the furnace roared—such a blaze you seldom see;
And I burrowed a hole in the glowing coal, and I stuffed in Sam McGee.

Then I made a hike; for I didn't like to hear him sizzle so;
And the heavens scowled, and the huskies howled, and the wind began to blow.
It was icy cold, but the hot sweat rolled down my cheeks, and I don't know why;
And the greasy smoke in an inky cloak went streaking down the sky.

I do not know how long in the snow I wrestled with grisly fear;
But the stars came out and they danced about ere again I ventured near;
I was sick with dread, but I bravely said: "I'll just take a peep inside.
I guess he's cooked, and it's time I looked", . . . then the door I opened wide.

And there sat Sam, looking cool and calm, in the heart of the
    furnace roar;
And he wore a smile you could see a mile, and he said: "Please
    close that door.
It's fine in here, but I greatly fear you'll let in the cold and
    storm—
Since I left Plumtree, down in Tennessee, it's the first time I've
    been warm."

There are strange things done in the midnight sun
    By the men who moil for gold;
The Arctic trails have their secret tales
    That would make your blood run cold;
The Northern Lights have seen queer sights,
    But the queerest they ever did see
Was that night on the marge of Lake Lebarge
    I cremated Sam McGee.

                  Robert Service

ACTIVITY: **Dramatisation**

Choose one of the poems in the unit to
dramatise in a small group or as a class.

I've Seen a Dreadful Thing . . .

The poems in this unit are all about ghosts.

The Glimpse

She sped through the door   1
And, following in haste,
And stirred to the core,
I entered hot-faced;
But I could not find her,   5
No sign was behind her.
'Where is she?' I said:
—'Who?' they asked that sat there;
'Not a soul's come in sight.'
—'A maid with red hair.'   10
—'Ah.' They paled. 'She is dead.
People see her at night,
But you are the first
On whom she has burst
In the keen common light.'   15

It was ages ago,
When I was quite strong:
I have waited since,—O,
I have waited so long!
—Yea, I set me to own   20
The house, where now lone
I dwell in void rooms
Booming hollow as tombs!
But I never come near her,

Though nightly, I hear her.   25
And my cheek has grown thin
And my hair has grown gray
With this waiting therein;
But she still keeps away!

Thomas Hardy

Who do you think *they* (line 8) are?
Why do you think the poet waits for the girl to come again?
What has slowly been happening to him?

Do you know of any real life ghost stories?

One of the most common features in ghost stories is that particular ghosts belong to particular places. They seem to cling after death to the places which were important to them in life.
The next poem is about a haunted wood.

The Way Through the Woods

They shut the road through the woods
Seventy years ago.
Weather and rain have undone it again,
And now you would never know
There was once a road through the woods
Before they planted the trees.
It is underneath the coppice and heath
And the thin anemones.
Only the keeper sees
That, where the ring-dove broods,
And the badgers roll at ease,
There was once a road through the woods.
Yet, if you enter the woods
Of a summer evening late,
When the night-air cools on the trout-ringed pools
Where the otter whistles his mate,
(They fear not men in the woods,
Because they see so few)
You will hear the beat of a horse's feet,
And the swish of a skirt in the dew,
Steadily cantering through
The misty solitudes,
As though they perfectly knew
The old lost road through the woods . . .
But there is no road through the woods.

Rudyard Kipling

Is there a way through the woods?
Who are *they* in the third line from the end?
Ghosts live in a cold, comfortless world of their
own. But suppose they want to leave their
world and enter ours?

Let Us In

'Let us in! Let us in!'
Who is crying above the wind's din?

'Let us in! Let us in!
We are pale and cold and thin.'

A clock chimes the midnight hour.
Are they creatures with magic power?

'Let us in! Let us in!
We are pale and cold and thin.'

They come and come and more and more.
Close the curtains! Lock the door!

'Let us in! Let us in!
We are pale and cold and thin.'

'Let us in! Let us in!
We are pale and cold and thin.'

Olive Dove

Who do you think *they* are? Why do they want
to get in?
Try letting one person read the narrator's part
in this poem while the rest of the class reads
the ghostly parts (in appropriate voices).

Why do you think all three poets have used
the vague word *they* in their poems, instead of
giving a more detailed description?

Prince Kano

In a dark wood Prince Kano lost his way
And searched in vain through the long summer's day.
At last, when night was near, he came in sight
Of a small clearing filled with yellow light,
And there, bending beside his brazier, stood
A charcoal burner wearing a black hood.
The Prince cried out for joy: 'Good friend, I'll give
What you will ask: guide me to where I live.'
The man pulled back his hood: he had no face—
Where it should be there was an empty space.

Half dead with fear the Prince staggered away,
Rushed blindly through the wood till break of day;
And then he saw a larger clearing, filled
With houses, people; but his soul was chilled,
He looked around for comfort, and his search
Led him inside a small, half-empty church
Where monks prayed. 'Father,' to one he said,
I've seen a dreadful thing; I am afraid.'
'What did you see, my son?' 'I saw a man
Whose face was like . . .' and, as the Prince began,
The monk drew back his hood and seemed to hiss,
Pointing to where his face should be, 'Like this?'

Edward Lowbury

Which ghost poem do you like best, and why?

ACTIVITY: **Taped Recitation and Sound Effects**

Work in groups of about four. Choose one or two of the poems to work on. Discuss and practise the best way of reading your poem(s) aloud. Work out good sound effects to go with your reading(s).
You can use voices or anything handy which will help give a spooky effect.
When you have perfected your presentation, some groups can perform for the class. You could also put some presentations on tape and play them for another class.

The Missing Link

The three poems in this unit have something in common. It isn't obvious what the link is and you may have to think quite hard to work it out.

Dust

Agatha Morley
All her life
Grumbled at dust
Like a good wife.

Dust on a table,
Dust on a chair,
Dust on a mantel
She couldn't bear.

She forgave faults
In man and child
But a dusty shelf
Would set her wild.

She bore with sin
Without protest,
But dust thoughts preyed
Upon her rest.

Agatha Morley
Is sleeping sound
Six feet under
The mouldy ground.

Six feet under
The earth she lies
With dust at her feet
And dust in her eyes.

Sydney King Russell

Spanish Waters

Spanish waters, Spanish waters, you are ringing in my
  ears,
Like a slow sweet piece of music from the grey forgotten
  years;
Telling tales, and beating tunes, and bringing weary
  thoughts to me
Of the sandy beach at Muertos, where I would that I
  could be.

There's a surf breaks on Los Muertos, and it never stops
  to roar,
And it's there we came to anchor, and it's there we
  went ashore,
Where the blue lagoon is silent amid snags of rotting
  trees,
Dropping like the clothes of corpses cast up by the seas.

We anchored at Los Muertos when the dipping sun was
  red,
We left her half-a-mile to sea, to west of Niger Head;
And before the mist was on the Cay, before the day was
  done,
We were all ashore on Muertos with the gold that we
  had won.

We bore it through the marshes in a half-score battered
  chests,
Sinking, in the sucking quagmires to the sunburn on our
  breasts,
Heaving over tree-trunks, gasping, damning at the flies
  and heat,
Longing for a long drink, out of silver, in the ship's cool
  lazareet.[1]

The moon came white and ghostly as we laid the
    treasure down,
There was gear there'd make a beggarman as rich as
    Lima Town,
Copper charms and silver trinkets from the chests of
    Spanish crews,
Gold doubloons and double moidores, louis d'ors
    and portagues,[2]

Clumsy yellow-metal earrings from the Indians of
    Brazil,
Uncut emeralds out of Rio, bezoar stones[3] from
    Guayaquil;
Silver, in the crude and fashioned[4], pots of old Arica
    bronze,
Jewels from the bones of Incas desecrated by the
    Dons.[5]

We smoothed the place with mattocks[6], and we took
    and blazed the tree,
Which marks yon where the gear is hid that none
    will ever see,
And we laid abroad the ship again, and south away
    we steers,
Through the loud surf of Los Muertos which is
    beating in my ears.

I'm the last alive that knows it. All the rest have
    gone their ways
Killed, or died, or come to anchor in the old
    Mulatas Cays,
And I go singing, fiddling, old and starved and in
    despair,

And I know where all that gold is hid, if I were only
    there.

It's not the way to end it all. I'm old, and nearly
    blind,
And an old man's past's a strange thing, for it never
    leaves his mind.
And I see in dreams, awhiles, the beach, the sun's disc
    dipping red,
And the tall ship, under topsails, swaying in past Niger
    Head.

I'd be glad to step ashore there. Glad to take a pick and
    go
To the lone blazed coco-palm tree in the place no others
    know,
And lift the gold and silver that has mouldered there
    for years
By the loud surf of Los Muertos which is beating in my
    ears.

John Masefield

1 *lazareet* – water container
2 *doubloons, moidores, louis d'ors, portagues* – European coins
3 *bezoar stones* – stony growths found in the stomachs of goats,
    antelopes, llamas, etc., formerly believed to be an antidote to
    all poisons.
4 *in the crude and fashioned* – unworked silver and things made
    out of silver
5 *bones of Incas desecrated by the Dons* – the Incas of Peru were
    wiped out by the Spanish invaders. Don is a Spanish title.
6 *mattocks* – pick-axes for loosening soil.

Pronunciation

Muertos – Mwer-tos	*portagues* – port-ag-use
Lima – Lee-ma	*louis d'ors* – loo-i-dors
moidores – moy-dors	*Guayaquil* – Guy-a-kill

Ozymandias of Egypt

I met a traveller from an antique land
   Who said: Two vast and trunkless legs of stone
Stand in the desert. Near them on the sand,
   Half sunk, a shatter'd visage lies, whose frown
And wrinkled lip and sneer of cold command
   Tell that its sculptor well those passions read
Which yet survive, stamp'd on these lifeless things,
   The hand that mock'd them and the heart that fed;
   And on the pedestal these words appear:
'My name is Ozymandias, king of kings:
   Look on my works, ye Mighty, and despair!'
Nothing beside remains. Round the decay
   Of that colossal wreck, boundless and bare,
The lone and level sands stretch far away.

Percy Bysshe Shelley

This is quite a difficult poem. These questions may help you understand what it is all about:
1. What did the traveller say that he saw standing in the desert?
2. What did he say he saw beside on the sand?
3. What was written on the base of the statue?
4. Why did these words strike the traveller as odd?

Can you see what the missing link is? What do the three poems have in common? When you have got an answer, turn to page 46 to see if you are thinking along the right lines.

Points of View

'Twixt optimist and pessimist
  The difference is droll
The optimist sees the doughnut
  The pessimist sees the hole.

Sometimes two people can look at the same problem or situation and see it very differently, as in the poem above. What is an optimist and what is a pessimist? Which are you?

In the next poem the planet Earth is being viewed through extra-terrestrial eyes.

Southbound on the Freeway

A tourist came in from Orbitville,
parked in the air, and said:

The creatures of this star
are made of metal and glass.

Through the transparent parts
you can see their guts.

Their feet are round and roll
on diagrams or long

measuring tapes, dark
with white lines.

They have four eyes.
The two in back are red.

Sometimes you can see a five-eyed
one, with a red eye turning

on the top of his head.
He must be special—

the others respect him
and go slow

when he passes, winding
among them from behind.

They all hiss as they glide,
like inches, down the marked

tapes. Those soft shapes,
shadowy inside

the hard bodies—are they
their guts or their brains?

May Swenson

What *are* the *creatures* the alien is looking at?
What other things on Earth do you think aliens would find peculiar?
What other things might they make mistakes about?

The next short poem is about two people viewing each other for the first time.

Double Negative

You were standing on the quay
Wondering who was the stranger on the mailboat
While I was on the mailboat
Wondering who was the stranger on the quay.

Richard Murphy

What do you think happened when the mailboat drew up on the quay?
How might the two people have met?

In the last two poems animals look at the world from their own viewpoints.

Fishes' Heaven

Fish (fly-replete, in depth of June,
Dawdling away their wat'ry noon)
Ponder deep wisdom, dark or clear,
Each secret fishy hope or fear.
Fish say, they have their Stream and Pond;
But is there anything Beyond?
This life cannot be All, they swear,
For how unpleasant, if it were!
One may not doubt that, somehow, Good
Shall come of Water and of Mud;
And, sure, the reverent eye must see
A Purpose in Liquidity.
We darkly know, by Faith we cry,
The future is not Wholly Dry.
Mud unto mud!—Death eddies near—
Not here the appointed End, not here!
But somewhere, beyond Space and Time,
Is wetter water, slimier slime!
And there (they trust) there swimmeth One.
Who swam ere rivers were begun,
Immense, of fishy form and mind,
Squamous[1], omnipotent, and kind;
And under that Almighty Fin,
The littlest fish may enter in.
Oh! never fly conceals a hook,
Fish say, in the Eternal Brook,
But more than mundane weeds are there,
And mud, celestially fair;
Fat caterpillars drift around,
And Paradisal grubs are found;
Unfading moths, immortal flies,
And the worm that never dies.
And in that Heaven of all their wish,
There shall be no more land, say fish.

Rupert Brooke

[1] *squamous* – covered in scales

Can you picture the fishes' heaven?
What sort of heaven might other animals long for?

Worms and the Wind

Worms would rather be worms.
Ask a worm and he says, "Who knows what a worm knows?"
Worms go down and up and over and under.
Worms like tunnels.
When worms talk they talk about the worm world.
Worms like it in the dark.
Neither the sun nor the moon interests a worm.
Zigzag worms hate circle worms.
Curve worms never trust square worms.
Worms know what worms want.
Slide worms are suspicious of crawl worms.
One worm asks another, "How does you belly drag today?"
The shape of a crooked worm satisfies a crooked worm.
A straight worm says, "Why not be straight?"
Worms tired of crawling begin to slither.
Long worms slither farther than short worms.
Middle-sized worms say, "It is nice to be neither long nor short."
Old worms teach young worms to say, "Don't be sorry for me unless you
   have been a worm and lived in worm places and read worm books."
When worms go to war they dig in, come out and fight, dig in again,
   come out and fight again, dig in again, and so on.
Worms underground never hear the wind overground and sometimes they
   ask, "What is this wind we hear of?"

Carl Sandburg

What is *Worms and the Wind* about?

ACTIVITY: Art

1. Paint or draw a picture inspired by one of the poems in the unit.

2. Design a travel poster for an Orbitville travel agent's office advertising weekend trips to Earth.

The Border Kipling

Will Ogilvie's poetry was very popular in its day, and reprinted many times, but it is nowadays rather hard to locate. Many of his Scottish poems were originally published in the Edinburgh *Evening News*.

Ogilvie wrote with great affection about his native border country. He was nicknamed ''the Border Kipling'', partly because – like Kipling – he wrote poetry about the outdoors life. Both poets too had close links with the old British Empire, Kipling with India, Ogilvie with Australia.

This memorial cairn to Will Ogilvie was erected on the moors beside his beloved hill road from Ashkirk to Roberton in 1993, thirty years after his death.

The poet with his wife and some of his family at home at Ashkirk, Selkirkshire, in 1949.

Will Ogilvie is perhaps better remembered as a poet in Australia than in his native Scotland. He wrote much poetry about life in the bush. You might be able to find the Australian collection *Saddle for a Throne* (1952, many reprints) in the library. A recent collection of his Scottish poetry is *The Border Poems of Will Ogilvie* (1992).

The Scotch Fir

This is the tallest tree within my woods,
Lean, rugged-stemmed, and of all branches bare
Full thirty feet, with green plumes in the air
And roots among the bracken. All his moods
Are rough but kingly; whether, grand, he broods
Above his full-leaved comrades in the glare
Of summer, or in winter, still more fair,
Nods princely time to the wind's interludes.
Beauty may claim the beeches, elm and oak
Stir sentiment in England; but the fir
Stands here for Scotland and the bleak brave North;
Too tall to stoop to any servile yoke,
Too strong of heart to more than lightly stir
When the worst storm-winds of the world break forth.

Will Ogilvie

This poem is in the form of a ''sonnet''. Sonnets
are poems of fourteen lines. They usually have a
certain rhyme-scheme, as in this poem, viz. a b b a
a b b a, followed by other rhymes in the last six
lines. There is usually a pause for thought after line
8 – description followed by comment.

On a Roman Helmet

A helmet of the legion, this,
That long and deep hath lain,
Come back to taste the living kiss
Of sun and wind again.
Ah! touch it with a reverent hand,
For in its burnished dome
Lies here within this distant land
The glory that was Rome!

The tides of sixteen hundred years
Have flowed, and ebbed, and flowed,
And yet – I see the tossing spears
Come up the Roman Road;
While, high above the trumpets pealed,
The eagles lift and fall,
And, all unseen, the War God's shield
Floats, guardian, over all!

Who marched beneath this gilded helm?
Who wore this casque a-shine?
A leader mighty in the realm?
A soldier of the line?
The proud patrician takes his rest
The spearman's bones beside,
And earth who knows their secret best
Gives this of all their pride!

With sunlight on this golden crest
Maybe some Roman guard,
Set free from duty, wandered west
Through Memory's gates unbarred;
Or climbing Eildon cleft in three,
Grown sick at heart for home,
Looked eastward to the grey North Sea
That paved the road to Rome.

Or by the queen of Border streams
That flowed his camp beneath
Long dallied with the dearer dreams
Of love as old as death,
And doffed this helm to dry lips' need,
And dipped it in the tide,
And pledged in brimming wine of Tweed
Some maid on Tiber-side.

Years pass; and Time keeps tally,
And pride takes earth for tomb,
And down the Melrose valley
Corn grows and roses bloom;
The red suns set, the red suns rise,
The ploughs lift through the loam,
And in one earth-worn helmet lies
The majesty of Rome.

Will Ogilvie

The Scottish Borders have yielded up lots of evidence of Roman activity. This is not really surprising, since the area was also a Roman frontier. "Eildon cleft in three" is a reference to the three peaks of the Eildon Hills above Melrose, and to the Roman fortress of Trimontium ("Three Mountains").

Scottish Rivers

The way of English rivers is a lazy winding way
Through marshes gold with buttercups and
    meadows sweet with hay;
The level land lies round them and their banks are
    broad and low,
And there is depth and stillness where the English
    rivers flow.

But our sturdy Scottish rivers, they come tumbling
    from the Bens
Like a crowd of happy children to make music in
    the glens;
The mountain mist surrounds them and the moorland
    heather flanks,
And the bending of the birches is a beauty on their
    banks.

They breast the barring boulders in their eagerness
    to be
The one before the other in the bosom of the sea;
They clutch the red scaur-edges and they trample
    down the clay,
And the thunder of their footsteps is a shout to
    clear the way.

The sparkling Scottish rivers when they win to open
    ground
Go tinkling through the lowlands over pebbles rolled
    and round,
Go laughing through the lowlands like the gipsy
    folk they are
Till they toss their white foam-garlands to the
    waves across the bar.

Will Ogilvie

scaur-edges: rock-faces, gullies

Ogilvie uses *alliteration* in his poetry, repeating
sounds at the beginning of words. Find examples
of this.

It is not only poets who are fond of alliteration;
advertisers use it too, as in ''Tetley tea totally
tantalises tastebuds''.

Think of some good alliterative sentences.

The First Blue Day on the Border

As I came over the Harden hill
A whaup on the moor was whistling shrill
In his pride to be first recorder
Of new life stirred in the sleeping ling,
Of laughter and love and song – and Spring –
And the first blue day on the Border.

As I came down on the Borthwick side
The thorn stood white as a waiting bride
And the willow was leaning toward her;
The song of the river was sweet and loud,
The sky had never a single cloud
On the first blue day on the Border.

The ash was jewelled with buds of jet,
The crimson tufts on the larch were set
To be lit when the gods gave order;
Over the elm was a ruby sheen
Where the sunlight glittered the boughs between
On the first blue day on the Border.

Will Ogilvie

ling: heather

The Road to Roberton

The hill road to Roberton: Ale Water at our feet,
And grey hills and blue hills that melt away and
   meet,
With cotton-flowers that wave to us and lone
   whaups that call,
And over all the Border mist – the soft mist over all.

When Scotland married England long, long ago,
The winds spun a wedding-veil of moonlight and
   snow,
A veil of filmy silver that sun and rain had kissed,
And she left it to the Border in a soft grey mist.

And now the dreary distance doth wear it like a
   bride,
Out beyond the Langhope Burn and over
   Essenside,
By Borthwick Wa's and Redfordgreen and on to
   wild Buccleuch
And up the Ettrick Water, till it fades into the blue.

The winding road to Roberton is little marked
   of wheels,
And lonely past Blawearie runs the track to
   Borthwickshiels,
Whitslade is slumbering undisturbed and down
   in Harden Glen
The tall trees murmur in their dreams of Wat's
   mosstrooping men.

A distant glint of silver, that is Ale's last goodbye,
Then Greatmoor and Windburgh against a purple sky,
The long line of the Carter, Teviotdale flung wide,
And a slight stir in the heather – a wind from the
    English side.

The hill road to Roberton's a steep road to climb,
But where your foot has crushed it you can smell
    the scented thyme,
And if your heart's a Border heart, look down to
    Harden Glen,
And hear the blue hills ringing with the restless
    hoofs again.

Will Ogilvie

whaups: curlews
Wat's mosstrooping men: Wat of Harden, like Tam Lin, was a fairy
figure from the myths and legends of the Border ballads.

Which of these poems by Will Ogilvie do you like
best? Why?
Why do you think Borderers are so proud of Will
Ogilvie?

ACTIVITY 1: **Art**
Make a recruiting poster for Roman soldiers on the
frontiers of the Empire. Try to make the work of
soldiering look attractive.

Or, make a tourist poster inviting visitors to explore
the Scottish Borders. Use some of Ogilvie's poetry
in your arrangement.

ACTIVITY 2: **Writing**
Try writing a sonnet in the style of *The Scotch Fir.*
Write about some feature of your own local
environment, or perhaps about someone you know
well.

UNIT NINE

My Mother Saw a Dancing Bear

The poems in this unit are about the relationship between animals and human beings. Sadly, this relationship is often soured by Man's cruelty. The first poem recalls the dancing bears which used to be trailed around the country as entertainment in Victorian and Edwardian times.

Musician and dancing bear in Edinburgh, 1908

My Mother Saw a Dancing Bear

My mother saw a dancing bear
By the schoolyard, a day in June.
The keeper stood with chain and bar
And whistle-pipe, and played a tune.

And bruin lifted up its head
And lifted up its dainty feet,
And all the children laughed to see
It caper in the summer heat.

They watched as for the Queen it died.
They watched it march. They watched it halt.
They heard the keeper as he cried,
"Now roly-poly!" "Somersault."

And then, my mother said, there came
The keeper with a begging cup,
The bear with burning coat of fur,
Shaming the laughter to a stop.

They paid a penny for the dance,
But what they saw was not the show;
Only, in bruin's aching eyes,
Far distant forests, and the snow.

Charles Causley

How old do you think the poet's mother was when she saw the dancing bear? Why do you think so?
The date of Charles Causley's birth is on page 11. Use it to work out roughly when his mother probably saw this happen.

Did the bear enjoy doing its act? How do you know?

Dancing bears are no longer allowed by law in Britain. Some people, however, feel that there are still many forms of legal cruelty to animals going on today.

Can you think of any? What do you feel about them?

The Snare

I hear a sudden cry of pain!
    There is a rabbit in a snare:
Now I hear the cry again,
    But I cannot tell from where.

But I cannot tell from where
    He is calling out for aid;
Crying on the frightened air,
    Making everything afraid,

Making everything afraid
    Wrinkling up his little face,
As he cries again for aid;
    —And I cannot find the place!

And I cannot find the place
    Where his paw is in the snare;
Little one! Oh, little one!
    I am searching everywhere!

James Stephens

What is a snare? Why do people use them? Do you approve or disapprove of them?

Look back to Unit One to refresh your memory about rhyme schemes. What is the rhyme scheme in *The Snare*?

A teacher once read *The Snare* to her class and they could not bear the ending. They insisted on composing a last verse in which the writer found and released the rabbit. Quickly try to do this. How would the last verse begin? (There is a definite pattern in the poem which means that there is no choice as to the first line of the verse.)

Poacher and gamekeeper

Adults were responsible for the misery of the dancing bear and the rabbit in the last two poems. But children can be cruel too.

Take One Home for the Kiddies

On shallow straw, in shadeless glass,
Huddled by empty bowls, they sleep:
No dark, no dam, no earth, no grass—
Mam, get us one of them to keep.

Living toys are something novel,
But it soon wears off somehow.
Fetch the shoebox, fetch the shovel—
Mam, we're playing funerals now.

Philip Larkin

There are two voices in the poem. The first three lines of each stanza require one type of voice, and the last lines, another. Work out the best way of reading it.
What sort of animals do you think the kiddies' pets were? Why do you think this?
What happened to them in the end? Why do you suppose this happened? Do you think the children meant to be cruel?
Are they to blame?

One of the good things about people is that they can sometimes see and understand what they have done wrong. In the next poem, the poet is asking for forgiveness for something he once did to hurt two living creatures.

Forgive My Guilt

Not always sure what things called sins may be,
I am sure of one sin I have done.
It was years ago, and I was a boy,
I lay in the frost flowers with a gun,
The air ran blue as the flowers, I held my breath,
Two birds on golden legs slim as dream things
Ran like quicksilver on the golden sand,
My gun went off, they ran with broken wings
Into the sea, I ran to fetch them in,
But they swam with their heads high out to sea,
They cried like two sorrowful high flutes,
With jagged ivory bones where wings should be.

For days I heard them when I walked that headland
Crying out to their kind in the blue,
The other plovers were going over south
On silver wings leaving these broken two.
The cries went out one day; but I still hear them
Over all the sounds of sorrow in war or peace
I ever have heard, time cannot drown them,
Those slender flutes of sorrow never cease.
Two airy things forever denied the air!
I never knew how their lives at last were spilt,
But I have hoped for years all that is wild,
Airy, and beautiful will forgive my guilt.

Robert P. Tristram Coffin

Do you think the poet meant to shoot the
birds?
What was it that made him realise the great
wrong that he had done?
What do you think is the saddest line in this
poem?
What occasions do you know of when an animal
has been hurt or harmed, by accident or on
purpose?
Which of these four poems do you like best?
Why?

Fabulous Steeds

For many thousands of years people have admired and loved horses for their beauty, strength and speed. The first poem in this unit is an extract from the Bible praising the horse.

The Horse

Hast thou given the horse strength?
Hast thou clothed his neck with thunder?
Canst thou make him afraid as a grasshopper?
The glory of his nostrils is terrible.
He paweth in the valley and rejoiceth in his strength:
He goeth to meet the armed men;
He mocketh at fear and is not affrighted,
Neither turneth he back from the sword.
The quiver rattleth against him,
The glittering spear and the shield—
He swalloweth the ground with fierceness and rage,
Neither believeth he that it is the sound of the trumpet—
He saith among the trumpets, "Ha! ha!"
And he smelleth the battle afar off,
The thunder of the captains, and the shouting.

From The Authorised Version

Job, 39

Study of horses, Leonardo da Vinci

Can you describe the horse in this extract in your own words?

The next poem also has links with long ago. It is about Pegasus, the winged horse from an Ancient Greek myth.

Pegasus

From the blood of Medusa
Pegasus sprang.
His hoof of heaven
Like melody rang.
His whinny was sweeter
Than Orpheus' lyre,
The wing on his shoulder
Was brighter than fire.

His tail was a fountain,
His nostrils were caves,
His mane and his forelock
Were musical waves.
He neighed like a trumpet,
He cooed like a dove,
He was stronger than terror
And swifter than love.

He could not be captured,
He could not be bought,
His rhythm was running,
His standing was thought.
With one eye on sorrow
And one eye on mirth
He galloped in heaven
And gambolled on earth.

And only the poet
With wings to his brain
Can mount him and ride him
Without any rein.
The stallion of heaven,
The steed of the skies,
The horse of the singer
Who sings as he flies.

Eleanor Farjeon

The poet uses many comparisons in her description of Pegasus. (Some of these are *metaphors*, where she makes the comparison by saying that one thing *is* another.)
Find the comparisons in the poem. Do you think they are appropriate? Why or why not? What does the poet mean when she says *Only the poet . . . can mount him and ride him* (last stanza)?

The next poem has a modern setting.

42

You'd Better Believe Him

He discovered an old rocking-horse in Woolworth's,
He tried to feed it but without much luck.
So he stroked it, had a long conversation about
The trees it came from, the attics it had visited.
Tried to take it out then
But the store detective he
Called the store manager who
Called the police who in court next morning said
'He acted strangely when arrested,
His statement read simply "I believe in rocking-horses."
We have reason to believe him mad.'
'Quite so,' said the prosecution,
'Bring in the rocking-horse as evidence.'
'I'm afraid it's escaped, sir,' said the store manager,
'Left a hoof-print as evidence
On the skull of the store detective.'
'Quite so,' said the prosecution, fearful
of the neighing
Out in the corridor.

Brian Patten

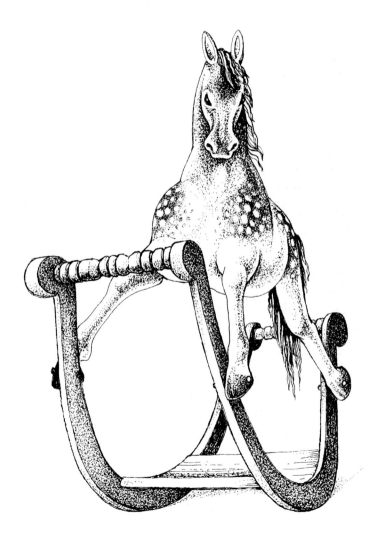

If someone opened the court-room door would
the horse be there? Why do you think so?

The last poem in this unit is about the world
after a nuclear war.

43

The Horses

Barely a twelvemonth after   1
The seven days war that put the world to sleep,
Late in the evening the strange horses came.
By then we had made our covenant with silence,
But in the first few days it was so still   5
We listened to our breathing and were afraid.
On the second day
The radios failed; we turned the knobs; no answer.
On the third day a warship passed us, heading north,
Dead bodies piled on the deck. On the sixth day   10
A plane plunged over us into the sea. Thereafter
Nothing. The radios dumb;
And still they stand in corners of our kitchens,
And stand, perhaps, turned on, in a million rooms
All over the world. But now if they should speak,   15
If on a sudden they should speak again,

If on the stroke of noon a voice should speak,
We would not listen, we would not let it bring
That old bad world that swallowed its children quick
At one great gulp. We would not have it again.   20
Sometimes we think of the nations lying asleep,
Curled blindly in impenetrable sorrow,
And then the thought confounds us with its strangeness.
The tractors lie about our fields; at evening
They look like dank sea-monsters couched and waiting.   25
We leave them where they are and let them rust:
"They'll moulder away and be like other loam."
We make our oxen drag our rusty ploughs,
Long laid aside. We have gone back
Far past our fathers' land.
                    And then, that evening   30
Late in the summer the strange horses came.

We heard a distant tapping on the road,
A deepening drumming; it stopped, went on again
And at the corner changed to hollow thunder.
We saw the heads   35
Like a wild wave charging and were afraid.
We had sold our horses in our fathers' time
To buy new tractors. Now they were strange to us
As fabulous steeds set on an ancient shield
Or illustrations in a book of knights.   40
We did not dare go near them. Yet they waited,
Stubborn and shy, as if they had been sent
By an old command to find our whereabouts
And that long-lost archaic companionship.
In the first moment we had never a thought   45
That they were creatures to be owned and used.
Among them were some half-a-dozen colts
Dropped in some wilderness of the broken world,
Yet new as if they had come from their own Eden.
Since then they have pulled our ploughs and borne our loads.   50
But that free servitude still can pierce our hearts.
Our life is changed; their coming our beginning.

Edwin Muir

The poem really starts in the middle of the story, when the horses arrive twelve months after the end of the war. Look back at the poem and retell the whole story in the order in which things happened. In what ways has the world changed because of the war? Why did the horses come and wait "stubborn and shy" (line 42)? Why do the horses seem so important to the survivors?

Do you think it might ever happen that the world will go back to a simple old-fashioned way of life? Or do you think the world will carry on getting more and more complicated, technological and "modern"?

ACTIVITY: **Drawing a Horse**

1. Lightly draw the lines of the head and neck. The lines are all curved.
   The neck is slightly longer and thicker than the head.

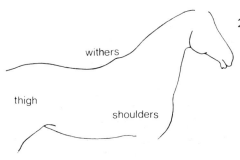

2. Next put in the shoulders and withers (a bulge at the base of the neck).
   The main part of a horse's body is called the 'barrel'.
   Again the lines have a slight curve. The horse's hip and thigh is very strong and broad.

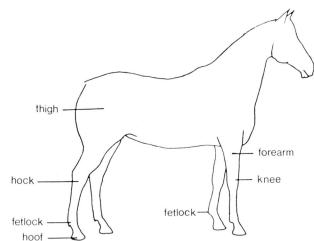

3. The horse's back leg curves out to the hockjoint (which is its heel). Then it goes straight down to the fetlock (toe-joint) and forward to the hoof.
   The horse's front leg comes straight down to the knee. The knee is a slight bulge, then the leg goes straight down again to the fetlock.

4. Lastly put in the details.
   The ears are on the top of the head (above the join of the neck and jaw). The eye is about a third of the way down the face.
   Put in the nostril, mouth, forelock and mane.
   The tail is a continuation of the spine, and is set quite high on the horse's rear end.

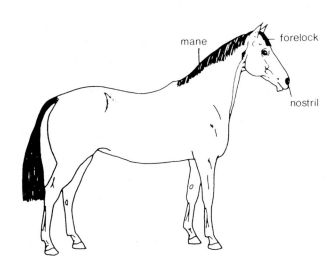

(Answer to question in Unit Six.)
The 'missing link' is *irony*. This is a situation in which someone seems to be mocked by the fates.
Agatha Morley spent her lifetime hating dust and now is buried in it; the pirate in *Spanish Waters* is blind and penniless – he knows where all the gold is hidden but he can't get it; Ozymandias tells everyone to gaze on his works and despair – but they have all crumbled to dust.

Biographical Notes on Poets

RUPERT BROOKE 1887 – 1915
Once called 'the handsomest young man in England'.
Became a poet while at Cambridge University before
the First World War. Was filled with a romantic and
patriotic desire to fight when war came. Enlisted. Died
of a mosquito bite on the lip while on active service in
the Greek islands.

THOMAS HARDY 1840 – 1928
Born and lived much of his life in Dorset. Delicate as a
boy. Learned French, Latin, German and Greek very
young. Trained as an architect but became writer of
novels and poems – very often with a country setting.
First novel was a (not very good) murder story. Most
famous later novel: *Tess of the d'Urbervilles* – a sad story
in which the heroine is hanged at the end.

RUDYARD KIPLING 1865 – 1936
Born in Bombay, India. After a happy early childhood
he was sent to school in Britain because of his health.
Was boarded out to people who treated him with great
cruelty and so frightened him that he told lies. He
resented this all his life. Returned to India at 17, where
he made his name as a writer. Won the Nobel Prize in
1907 for his novels and poetry. His most famous stories
for children are *The Jungle Books* and *The Just So
Stories*.

EDWIN MUIR 1887 – 1959
Born in Orkney but was moved as a teenager to the
worst slums of Glasgow. Suffered a dreadful shock and
the horror of what he saw there lasted all his life. Never
forgot the horses he knew in his childhood. They
always had a magical significance for him. A quiet,
gentle man who wrote poems and novels.

WILLIAM HENRY OGILVIE 1869 – 1963
Born near Kelso, in the Scottish Borders, Ogilvie grew
up on his parents' farm. After school in Edinburgh, he
was sent to work as a cattle-rancher and horse-breaker
in the Australian outback. He lived "down under" and
knew Banjo Paterson, of *Waltzing Matilda* fame. He
knocked about the bush for 12 years, before returning
to Scotland to live near Selkirk. His poetry and songs
had a huge public following in his day, and he is one of
the few poets this century to have earned a good

livelihood from his pen. The critics were always rather sniffy about him.

WILFRED OWEN AND SIEGFRIED SASSOON
Wilfred Owen was born in 1893. He fought in the 1914–18 war and was awarded the Military Cross for bravery. Owen found the war and the suffering of his fellow soldiers disgusting and horrifying. He wrote many poems about the horrors of war. Killed in action in 1918. Siegfried Sassoon (nicknamed "Mad Jack" for his recklessness) also wrote war poetry from the trenches, but survived the war. Died in 1967.

ROBERT SERVICE 1874 – 1958
Born in Preston, Lancashire. Educated in Glasgow. Worked in a bank. Emigrated to Canada at 21 and spent eight years in a bank in the Yukon. Later became a reporter and an ambulance driver in the 1914–18 war. Famous for verses about the Yukon in books such as *Rhymes of a Rolling Stone*.

PERCY BYSSHE SHELLEY 1792 – 1822
Born into a wealthy family. Educated at Eton, where he was known as "Mad Shelley". He was bullied at school and because of this hated violence all his life. Was sent down from Oxford at 18 and eloped at 19 and again later in life. A hasty and tempestuous man, full of wild schemes which didn't come off. Wrote some of the best poetry ever written in English. Drowned when his boat capsized, aged only 30. His wife, Mary Shelley, wrote the novel *Frankenstein*.

Acknowledgements

Thanks are due to the following publishers, agents and authors for permission to reprint the material indicated. Every effort has been made to trace copyright but if any omissions have been made please let us know in order that we may put it right in the next edition.

George Allen & Unwin for 'You'd Better Believe Him' by Brian Patten from *Little Johnny's Confession*.
B. D. Bartlett for 'Let Us In' by Olive Dove.
Mrs. Robert P. T. Coffin for 'Forgive My Guilt' by Robert P. Tristram Coffin. Reprinted by kind permission.
Faber & Faber Ltd. for 'Take One Home for the Kiddies' by Philip Larkin from *The Whitsun Weddings*; 'The Horses' by Edwin Muir.
Harcourt, Brace, Jovanovich Inc. for 'Worms and the Wind' by Carl Sandburg from *Complete Poems*.
David Higham Associates Ltd. for 'My Neighbour Mr Normanton' and 'Cowboy Song' by Charles Causley from *Union Street*, Macmillan; 'I Saw a Jolly Hunter', 'Infant Song' and 'My Mother Saw a Dancing Bear' by Charles Causley from *Collected Poems*, Macmillan; 'Pegasus' by Eleanor Farjeon; The Estate of Robert Service for 'The Creation of Sam McGee' by Robert Service. Reprinted by permission.
Edward Lowbury for 'Prince Kano' from *Green Magic*, Chatto and Windus.
The National Trust for Places of Historic Interest or Natural Beauty and Macmillan, London Ltd. for 'The Way Through the Woods' by Rudyard Kipling from *The Definitive Edition of Rudyard Kipling's Verse*. Reprinted by kind permission.
George T. A. Ogilvie for 'The Scotch Fir', 'On a Roman Helmet', 'Scottish Rivers', 'The First Blue Day on the Border', and 'The Road to Roberton', all by Will Ogilvie. Reprinted by kind permission.
George Sassoon for 'The General' by Siegfried Sassoon from *Complete Poems*, Faber. Reprinted by permission.
The Society of Authors as the literary representative of the Estate of John Masefield for 'Spanish Waters' and 'Sea Fever' by John Masefield; The Society of Authors on behalf of the copyright owner, Mrs. Iris Wise for 'The Snare' by James Stephens.

We are grateful to the following for assistance in finding photographs: BBC Hulton Picture Library pp. 7, 8, 9 & 10; Mrs. Scott p. 37; Mary Evans Picture Library p. 38; J. Allan Cash pp. 37, 44 & 45; Royal Library, Windsor Castle. By gracious permission of H.M. The Queen p. 41.